China

Gisela Lee, M.A.

Publishing Credits

Associate Editor
Christina Hill, M.A.

Assistant Editor
Torrey Maloof

Editorial Assistants
Deborah Buchana
Kathryn R. Kiley
Judy Tan

Editorial Director
Emily R. Smith, M.A.Ed.

Editor-in-Chief
Sharon Coan, M.S.Ed.

Creative Director
Lee Aucoin

Cover Designer
Lesley Palmer

Designers
Deb Brown
Zac Calbert
Amy Couch
Robin Erickson
Neri Garcia

Publisher
Rachelle Cracchiolo, M.S.Ed.

Teacher Created Materials

5301 Oceanus Drive
Huntington Beach, CA 92649
http://www.tcmpub.com
ISBN 978-0-7439-0436-0

Table of Contents

China's Changing History

China is located in Southeast Asia. It borders 14 other countries. Beijing (BAY-jing) is its capital city. China is home to the world's largest human-made structure, the Great Wall of China. It is the fourth largest country in the world. The Himalaya (hih-muh-LAY-uh) Mountains and Yangtze (YANG-see) River are important to China's geography. Today, there are over a billion Chinese people in the world.

At first, kings ruled ancient China. These men fought one another over land and resources. Then, **emperors** ruled China. They ruled in families called **dynasties** (DI-nuhs-teez).

Early in the twentieth century, the dynasty system collapsed. China did not have a stable government. Then, China became a republic. Finally, a **communist** (KAWM-yuh-nist) government was formed.

▼ The Great Wall of China is often crowded with tourists.

4

▲ China today

Incredible Inventions

Civilizations (siv-uh-luh-ZAY-shuhnz) in China have been around for thousands of years. The Chinese made many important contributions. They invented the crossbow, gunpowder, magnetic compass, kite, wheelbarrow, and paper.

Many Different Chinese People

The people in China come from more than 55 different **ethnic** groups.

▼ The people in China are very diverse.

5

Prehistoric China

The first Chinese civilization was in the Yellow River Valley. It was part of the Xia (she-AH) dynasty. The Xia ruled from about 2000 to 1600 B.C.

King Qi (CHI) established a **hereditary** (huh-RED-uh-tair-ee) system of leadership. That means that the new ruler was always related to the previous one. A king's son usually became the next king. The Shang tribe overthrew this dynasty around 1600 B.C.

There were many lakes and marshes in ancient China. The first farmers settled along the Yellow River. Pottery and silk were important products made during this era. The geography of China kept it separate from other civilizations in the world. So, there was not a lot of trade during this time.

▼ Yellow River Valley

▲ Chinese farming today

Farming in China Today

Farming is still important to the Chinese economy. China is a leading producer of wheat, rice, corn, tea, and barley.

Still Important Silk

Silk is still an export in China today. It makes up a part of China's **textile** (TEKS-tile) industry. Silk is used to make clothing and other products around the world. Not many people outside of China knew how to make silk until the 800s.

Shang Dynasty

The Shang dynasty was in power from around 1600 to 1046 B.C. This dynasty is best known for its work with bronze. But, people in this dynasty also provided the most complete record of early China. The oldest writings of Chinese civilization came from this time. These writings were carved onto animal shells and bones. These are often referred to as **oracle** (OR-uh-kuhl) **bones**.

Oracle ▶ bones tell the early history of China.

Farming was advanced by the use of stone plows. The first towns and cities were built in China during the Shang dynasty. Towns were often divided into wards. The sections were separated by walls. Different groups of people lived in each ward.

Silk or Metal?

Many bronze **artifacts** exist today from the Shang dynasty. It is clear they were excellent metalworkers. However, they were also skilled with silk. The silk industry grew during the Shang dynasty. Soon, this expensive thread was in great demand.

Oracle Bones

Archaeologists (awr-key-AWL-uh-jists) have been busy in China. Since the beginning of the nineteenth century, there have been over 100,000 pieces of animal shells or bones discovered. These are being studied. This is how people today learn about the early Chinese civilizations.

◀ Bronze work from the Shang dynasty

Long-Lasting Zhou Dynasty

The Zhou (JO) dynasty was the longest dynasty in Chinese history. It lasted about 900 years. They were in power from around 1046 to 221 B.C. This was the first dynasty to keep written records of what happened on a daily basis.

This dynasty was divided into two time periods. First, there was the Western Zhou. It existed from about 1046 to 771 B.C. Next, came the Eastern Zhou. They were in power from around 771 to 221 B.C. The names are based on where the capital city was located.

The emperors during the late Zhou dynasty were not very strong. They could not control their people. So, many smaller states were formed. The armies of the states fought against one another. Soon, civil war erupted. There were many long battles. Thousands of men died. And, the countryside was destroyed.

The decline of the Zhou dynasty was the beginning of major social changes in China. A great age of **philosophy** (fuh-LAWS-uh-fee) was about to begin.

◀ Empress Wu of the Zhou dynasty

Dividing the Eastern Zhou

To make it even more confusing, the Eastern Zhou had two shorter periods. The Spring and Autumn period was first. It lasted for almost 300 years. The Warring States period was about the last 250 years of the Zhou dynasty.

Powerful Iron

Iron was a very valuable metal. It made plows stronger. Weapons could be also strengthened. Men at war wore iron armor to protect themselves. Iron is still a valuable resource across the world today.

◀ These are bells created during the Warring States period.

Philosophies in China

Life in China was uncertain. The wars were hard on people. Three new philosophies began during this time period. The leaders of these philosophies believed that peace was more important than war. Each philosophy left a lasting impression on Chinese civilization.

A man named Confucius (kuhn-FYOO-shuhs) was the most famous philosopher. His teachings are the basis for Confucianism (kuhn-FYOO-shuhn-izuhm). He believed that the family was more important than anything else. He thought that fathers should rule the families. And, that kings should rule the country. Confucius taught that everyone had a place in society. It was everyone's moral duty to obey the rulers.

Taoism (DAU-izuhm) was founded by Laozi (LAUD-zuh). He believed that people should learn from nature. Nature has everything right. People should not be forced to follow rules set up by men. They should follow rules set up by nature.

The third philosophy was Legalism (LEE-guhl-izuhm). This was based on the beliefs of Xunzi (shuhn-ZEH). Legalists thought that life should be controlled through discipline and laws.

Laozi founded ▶
Taoism.

◀ Confucius was an important philosopher.

◀ People study and worship Confucius at this temple.

Confucianism Today

Confucianism is still widely practiced throughout many countries in Asia. People in Korea and Japan have built temples to honor this philosophy.

The Way of Taoism

The word *tao* (DAU) means "The Way." The Way is the path to happiness. Taoists believe their path to happiness is to lead simple lives. They do not try to get rich or famous.

Short, but Sweet: The Qin Dynasty

Qin Shi Huang

After the fall of the Zhou dynasty, the Qin (CHIN) dynasty took over. This dynasty only lasted about 15 years. But, it was a very important dynasty. The first emperor of China led during this dynasty.

Qin Shi Huang (CHIN SHE HWANG) was the first emperor. He unified the country. He brought the country together by ending the constant battles. Qin now controlled all the regions of China.

Over the years, other leaders had built walls to protect China. Emperor Qin decided to connect these walls and make them larger. This was the start of what would become the Great Wall of China.

▼ The Great Wall of China

▲ Terra-cotta soldiers

Qin believed he was a very important man. So, he wanted to have a tomb that would show how powerful he was. He had artists create over 7,000 **terra-cotta** (tear-ruh-KAWT-tuh) soldiers. These soldiers would stand guard over him after he died.

Emperor Qin set a single system of weights and measures. He made written language more uniform. The emperor also made sure that roads and canals were built to connect one town to the next. Qin even formed a centralized government. That is a lot to get done in such a short time.

Terra-cotta Army

The 7,400 terra-cotta soldiers were discovered in 1974. These statues provide important information about warfare during ancient times.

The Great Wall

Did you know that the Great Wall of China is not one long wall? Overall, it's over 4,000 miles (6,000 km) long. But, all of the sections are not connected.

Land under the rule
of the Han Dynasty

Current boundaries
of China and Mongolia

N
W E
S

HAN

Emperor
Han Wu

The Prosperous Han Dynasty

After Emperor Qin died, his sons could not keep control of the country. Soon, the Han (HAWN) dynasty began. This dynasty was one of the strongest in Chinese history. It lasted from 206 B.C. to A.D. 220.

During the Han dynasty, China was the largest country in the world. There were about 60 million people living there.

The great Silk Road was formed during this time. This trade route went from China to Europe. It was the first major link between Asia and the countries in Europe.

This is a map of the land controlled by the Han dynasty overlayed on China today.

Papermaking, the crossbow, and the **seismograph** (SIZE-muh-graf) were all invented. The first Chinese dictionary was printed in A.D. 100. The Han dynasty was a time of great advances for China.

Once the powerful Han dynasty fell, there were many wars that followed. Different kingdoms controlled various parts of southern China. **Barbarians** (bawr-BER-ee-uhnz) controlled the north.

▼ Traders travel along the Silk Road.

Two Chinese Dynasties

China was reunited during the Sui (SWAY) dynasty (A.D. 581–618). There were great advances in transportation during this time. Also, iron chains were used to create suspension bridges. That made it easier to cross wide rivers.

Confucianism became a large part of Chinese culture. Another philosophy was introduced during this time. It was called **Buddhism** (BOO-dih-zuhm). Buddhist monks from India introduced this philosophy to the Chinese.

◀ Rubbing of Chinese calligraphy

This is a statue of the founder of Buddhism. ▶

There were many cultural developments during the Tang (TAWNG) dynasty (A.D. 618–907). Around A.D. 700, the Chinese started to print on carved, wooden blocks. They also created beautiful painted pictures on silk scrolls. These scrolls showed the rural and industrial culture of this time.

▼ The Grand Canal connected two important rivers in China.

Buddhism in Asia

Buddhism is still practiced in China today. China is a country without an official religion. However, Buddhism is still tied to traditional Chinese culture. It is also widely practiced in other Asian countries.

China's Grand Canal

The Grand Canal connected the Yangtze River to the Yellow River. It became the longest human-made canal in China. Extensions have been added to the Grand Canal over time. It now connects China's four major rivers. The Chinese use the canal for moving goods throughout China.

The Mongols Conquer China

▲ Genghis Khan led the Mongols.

The Mongols (MAWN-guhlz) were invaders who conquered China. They attacked after the fall of the Song (SOUNG) dynasty. They were in control of China from A.D. 1279 to 1368.

A man named Genghis Khan (jen-guhs-KAWN) began the Yuan (YWAWN) dynasty. Khan was the first ruler of China who was not Chinese. The Mongols controlled much of eastern Europe as well as China.

During this time, outsiders freely traveled to and from China. People from all over the world visited the country. Marco Polo was an Italian merchant. He lived in Venice, Italy. Polo visited China. In fact, he even advised Khan. He stayed in China from 1275 to 1292. Later, Polo wrote about his experiences in a book.

◀ Two characters from a modern Chinese opera

▲ A page from Marco Polo's book, *The Travels of Marco Polo*

Chinese Opera

The Chinese opera was called the *ju*. It was very important to the Chinese people. Today, it is still an important part of Chinese culture. Many operas from the past are still performed. They tell stories of different historical periods. The operas are very powerful musically and visually.

Marco Polo's Influence

Many people in the world read Polo's book. One person who read it was Christopher Columbus. The stories about Asia inspired Columbus. He wanted to see all the wonderful sites that Polo described.

The Brilliant Ming Dynasty

A man named Zhu Yuanzhang (JOO you-AHN-jahng) led a revolt. He overthrew the Mongols. Then, he became the emperor. A Chinese ruler was in charge of the country again. This was the beginning of the Ming dynasty.

The Forbidden City was built during this time. This was the home of the Chinese emperor and his family. It took more than 10 years to build. A wide moat and a high wall surround it. It was called The Forbidden City because commoners were not allowed inside the red walls.

This dynasty started many libraries. As more people learned to read and write, more novels were written and printed. Some of these novels would become classical literature. During the final years of the Ming dynasty, European ships landed on China's shores.

Tombs of the Ming Dynasty

The Ming rulers wanted incredible tombs. They wanted to be honored and protected in death. The Sacred Way is the road leading to their tombs. Along the Sacred Way are carved animals. The rulers believed these animals would always protect them.

Not Forbidden Anymore

Anyone can visit The Forbidden City today. It is located in Beijing. This historic site is one of the most popular tourist attractions in the world.

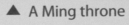
▲ A Ming throne

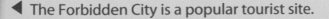
◄ The Forbidden City is a popular tourist site.

The Last Chinese Dynasty

Empress Tzu Shi

The Qing (CHING) dynasty ruled for over 200 years. This dynasty is also called the Manchu (MAN-choo) dynasty. They were in power from 1644 to 1911. This was the last dynasty to rule China. The first and only empress ruled China during the Qing dynasty. Her name was Tzu Shi (TSOO SHEE).

During this era, China expanded its territory. It included Manchuria (man-CHUR-ee-uh), Mongolia (mawn-GO-lyuh), Tibet (tuh-BET), and Taiwan (TIE-wawn). By this time, Europeans were trading with China.

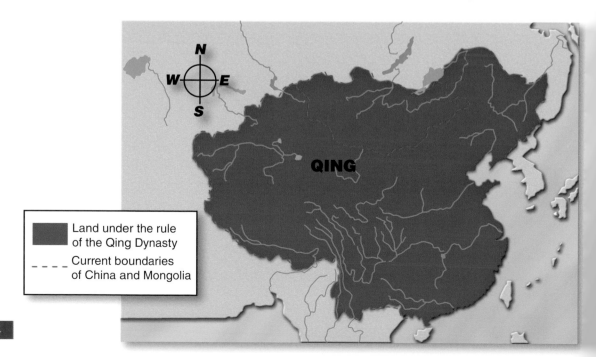

N
W E
S

QING

Land under the rule of the Qing Dynasty

Current boundaries of China and Mongolia

But, there was only one port open for trading. And, China did not import many goods.

Europeans did not like being limited in how much they could trade with China. The Treaty of Nanking forced China to open more ports.

The forced trading weakened the Chinese economy. Soon, the Taiping Rebellion (TIE-ping rih-BEL-yuhn) took place. This would begin a series of **rebellions**. The rebellions led to the end of the dynasties in China.

Trade: Good or Bad?

Foreign trade weakened China, but it was very important, too. Trade is now the backbone of China's economy. Without it, China's manufacturing industries would be smaller. In fact, the global economy would be impacted. The people of China are large consumers and producers of goods.

Hong Kong

The Treaty of Nanking was not fair to the Chinese. Foreign trade was forced on them. And, Hong Kong became a British colony. That means Great Britain controlled the city. Hong Kong stayed a colony until the end of the twentieth century.

◀ Hong Kong Harbor today

Modern China

The Republic of China was founded in 1912. That was after an event called the Boxer Rebellion. The Boxer Rebellion is what led to the downfall of the last dynasty. After this rebellion, the country became a **republic**. And, a president was elected.

There were two powerful groups in the Republic of China. The Nationalist Party wanted a unified China. They were also called the Kuomintang (kwo-MIN-tang). This group believed people should have some control over their lives. The other group was the Communist Party. A man named Mao Zedong (MAO zuh-DONG) led the Communist Party. He believed the government should be in control.

In 1934, an army of communist soldiers fought against the nationalists. After a deadly **civil war**, the communists won. They took over the mainland of China. By 1949, Zedong was in power. He formed the People's Republic of China. This is a communist government.

▲ Chiang Kai-shek led the Nationalist Party.

Modern China is an industrial nation backed by a large military force. Chinese people are not isolated from the outside world as their ancestors were. Today, they want to know and learn about the global community. And, they are proud of what China has become today.

Sun Yat-sen

Mao Zedong ▶ was the leader of the communists.

Father of Modern China

Sun Yat-sen (SUN YAWT-sen) was an important political leader. He led his people against the last dynasty. He knew that his country needed stability. He was elected the first president of the Republic of China. He also worked with Chiang Kai-shek (JE-awng KYE-shek) to lead the Nationalist Party.

Honoring Mao Zedong

Mao Zedong's beliefs are the foundation of the current political system of China. There are many statues and memorials in honor of Zedong throughout China.

China's Influence

China is a country that is tied to its culture. But, it is also trying to embrace the changes of modern times. The growth of manufacturing and industry contributed to China's economy. So did farming and fishing. Today, many products that are purchased around the world are made in China.

▼ Hong Kong is an important industrial city in China.

China has not forgotten to take care of nature and the land. China is home to over 100 species of rare and endangered animals. It has over 600 nature reserves.

Chinese people celebrate the growth of their nation. It reflects their place in the world.

Women in China

The role of women in Chinese society today is important. Chinese women are no longer thought of as less important than men. Chinese women are a significant part of today's work force. Their contributions have become more recognized and valued.

▲ Panda bears are one of the endangered animals living in China.

Glossary

archaeologists—people who study the past through artifacts

artifacts—objects made by people in past times

barbarians—term used for anyone who was not of Chinese descent

Buddhism—religion that believes that there is suffering in life and you can find a middle ground to escape the suffering

civil war—war between people living in the same country

civilizations—societies that have writing and keep track of records

communist—person who believes that everyone should share belongings and the government should control production

dynasties—family groups that maintain control or power for many generations

emperors—leaders of a dynasty or rulers of an empire

ethnic—relating to people from a similar race, country, or background

hereditary—passed down from family members through the generations

oracle bones—early writings created by people in China; writings were on bones and shells of animals

philosophy—belief system or ideas

rebellions—fights against the people in control

republic—a type of government that is led by an elected president or leader who is not a monarch

seismograph—instrument for measuring and recording the vibrations of the earth

terra-cotta—baked-clay materials used to make tools, statues, and pottery during early Chinese history

textile—cloth or fibers used to make cloth

Index

Image Credits